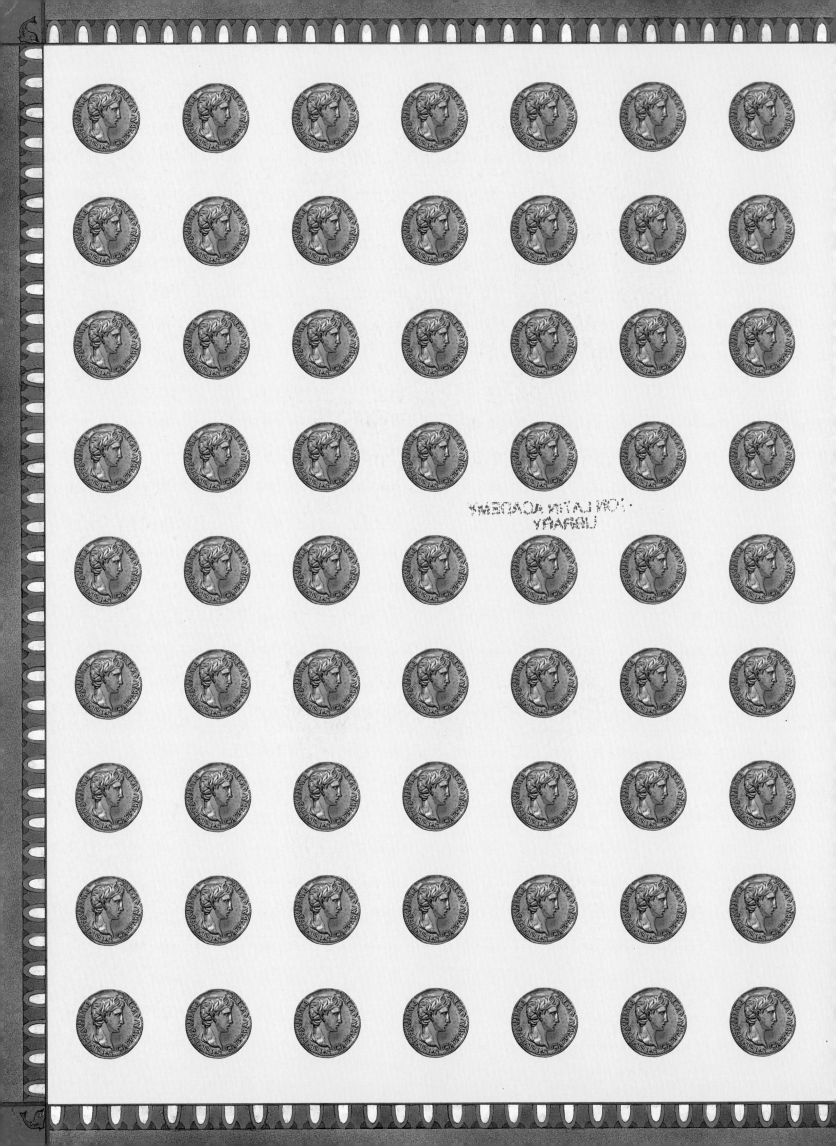

the world of the
R·O·M·A·N
EMPEROR

Peter Chrisp

Illustrations by
Studio Galante

PETER BEDRICK BOOKS
NEW YORK

For Lisa
(P.C.)

Published in the United States in 1999
by Peter Bedrick Books
A division of NTC/Contemporary
Publishing Group Inc
4255 West Touhy Avenue
Lincolnwood (Chicago) Illinois 60646-1975
U.S.A.

Text and illustrations
© 1999 Macdonald Young Books,
an imprint of Wayland Publishers Limited

Commissioning editor: Dereen Taylor
Editor: Ruth Thomson
Designer: Edward Kinsey

Chrisp, Peter.
The World of the Roman Emperor/Peter Chrisp
p.   cm.
Summary: Describes life in ancient Rome and
the succession of emperors, from Pompey to
Justinian, who ruled this empire.
ISBN 0-87226-296-0 (hardcover)
1. Emperors--Rome--Biography Juvenile
literature. 2. Rome--Army--Political activity
Juvenile literature. 3. Rome--Politics and
government--30 B.C.-476 A.D.--Pictorial works
Juvenile literature. 4. Rome--Civilisation--
Pictorial works Juvenile literature
[1. Rome--Civilisation. 2. Kings, queens, rulers,
etc.] I. Title.
DG274 C48 1999
937 06 0922--dc21
[ ]   99-25317
CIP

Printed and bound in Portugal
by Edicoes ASA

International Standard Book Number:
0-87226-296-0

99 00 01 02 03 15 14 13 12 11 10 9 8
7 6 5 4 3 2 1

4

PETER CHRISP

Peter Chrisp is an experienced author
of children's history books, who has
already written several books on the
Romans. His fascination with Ancient
Rome began as a small child, when he
refused to go anywhere without
wearing his plastic Roman breastplate
and helmet, with red feather plumes.
He has an M.A. in English Literature
from London University.

STUDIO GALANTE

Formed in 1995 and based in Florence,
Italy, Studio Galante consists of four
young illustrators – L. R. Galante,
Manuela Cappon, Francesco Spadoni
and Alessandro Menchi. The studio
has an international reputation for
illustrating historical reference books
for children and young adults.

CONTENTS

INTRODUCTION

ROMAN TERRITORY IN 50 BC

Success in war gave Roman generals, such as Julius Caesar, great opportunities for power and wealth. Each man wanted to outdo his rivals, and his own ancestors, in conquering new territory for Rome.

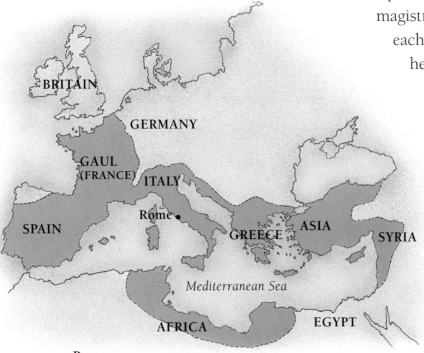

By the end of the first century BC, the world ruled by Rome was vast. The Empire included most of the lands around the Mediterranean Sea. At the time, the Romans had no single ruler. In 510 BC, the Romans had driven out their last king and invented a system designed to stop any one man becoming too powerful. This was called a Republic. Instead of a king, there were two chief magistrates, called consuls, who were elected each year by the citizens. These consuls were heads of government and commanders of the armies. They presided over the Senate, an assembly of 600 wealthy ex-magistrates. In theory, the Senate was there to advise the two elected consuls. In practice, the Senate made most of the important decisions, such as declaring war, or creating laws.

Pompey

Julius Caesar

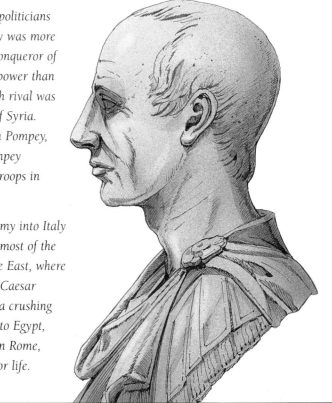

CIVIL WAR

Rome's consuls were ambitious politicians who were also generals. Nobody was more ambitious than Julius Caesar, conqueror of Gaul. He wanted more lasting power than being consul for a year. His arch rival was Pompey the Great, conqueror of Syria. In 49 BC, Caesar quarreled with Pompey, who dominated the Senate. Pompey ordered Caesar to disband his troops in Gaul and return to Rome.

Instead, Caesar marched his army into Italy and seized power. Pompey and most of the senators had already left for the East, where they gathered their own forces. Caesar followed and, in 48 BC, he won a crushing victory in Greece. Pompey fled to Egypt, where he was murdered. Back in Rome, Caesar made himself dictator for life.

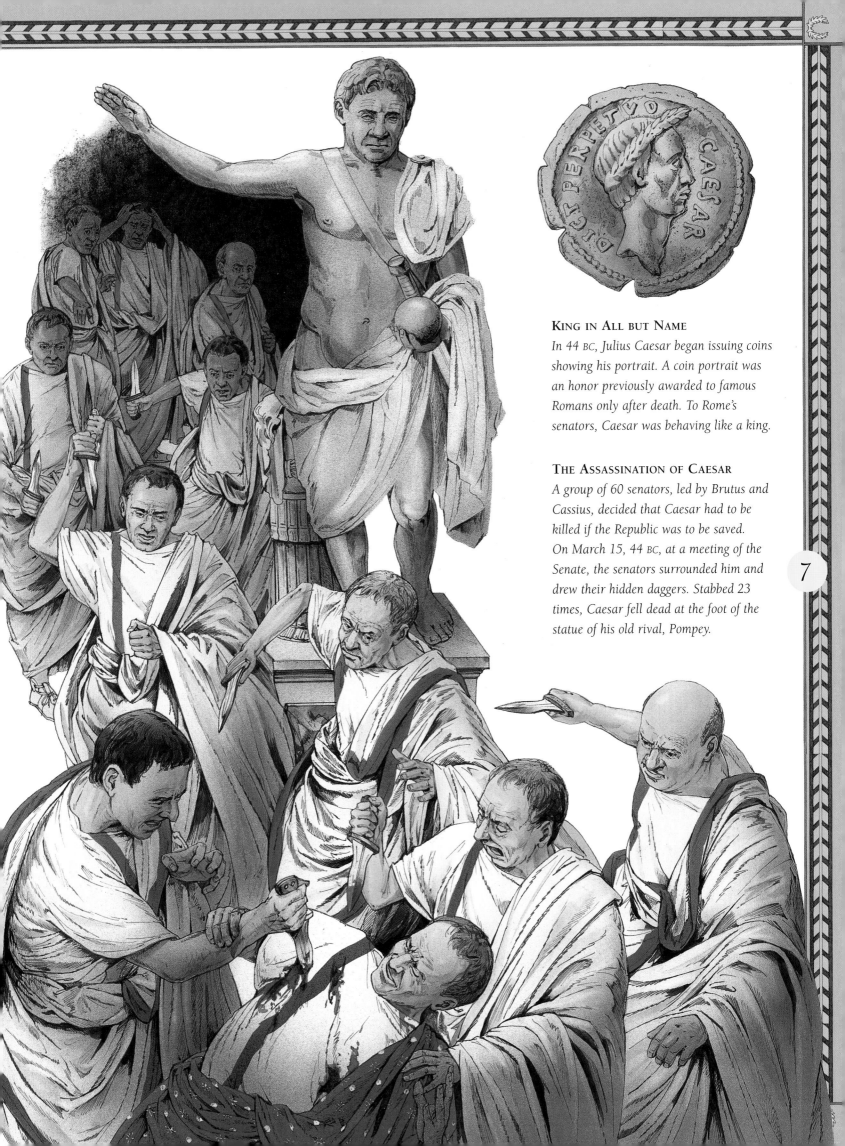

KING IN ALL BUT NAME

In 44 BC, Julius Caesar began issuing coins showing his portrait. A coin portrait was an honor previously awarded to famous Romans only after death. To Rome's senators, Caesar was behaving like a king.

THE ASSASSINATION OF CAESAR

A group of 60 senators, led by Brutus and Cassius, decided that Caesar had to be killed if the Republic was to be saved. On March 15, 44 BC, at a meeting of the Senate, the senators surrounded him and drew their hidden daggers. Stabbed 23 times, Caesar fell dead at the foot of the statue of his old rival, Pompey.

OCTAVIAN AND ANTONY

After defeating Caesar's assassins, Antony and Octavian shared the Roman Empire between them. To make their alliance firmer, Antony married Octavian's sister, Octavia. The alliance broke down when Antony fell in love with Cleopatra, Queen of Egypt, and divorced Octavia to marry her.

ANTONY'S SUICIDE

In 31 BC, Octavian defeated Antony and Cleopatra at the battle of Actium, and pursued them to Egypt. Antony asked for peace, but Octavian ordered him to commit suicide. Antony stabbed himself inside his Egyptian tomb. Octavian inspected the corpse to make sure his enemy was really dead.

AUGUSTUS

The assassination of Caesar did not save the Republic. It only led to further civil war. Caesar's adopted son, a 19-year-old called Octavian, raised an army and marched on Rome. With Caesar's lieutenant, Mark Antony, he began a war against Brutus and Cassius and, in 42 BC, defeated them at the battle of Philippi in Macedonia. The two men divided the Empire – Octavian took the west and Antony the east. Before long, they too began to fight with each other. Antony lost this war and killed himself in 30 BC, leaving Octavian as sole ruler of the Roman world. Three years later, Octavian announced that he was giving power back to the Senate, claiming that he was now only the *princeps* (first citizen) in a restored Republic. In reality, his power was total. He decided who belonged to the Senate. He was commander-in-chief of the army. Renamed Augustus (the honored one), Octavian had become Rome's first emperor.

THE REPUBLIC RESTORED

In 27 BC, Octavian, now called Augustus, amazed Rome's senators by telling them that he was giving up his powers and restoring the Republic. However, it soon became clear that Augustus was giving up very little. Senators were allowed to administer peaceful provinces, but Augustus kept control of the troubled frontiers, where Rome's armies were based. The result was that only Augustus had any armies under his command. The Senate had few political powers, but Augustus made sure that it kept its traditional prestige.

MORNING AUDIENCE

Ruthless in his rise to power, Augustus showed a different side once he had gained it. Unlike Caesar, he did not behave like a king. Every morning, in his home, Augustus received visitors who came with requests. He gave them all a friendly reception and made them feel at ease.

THE CITY OF ROME

Augustus began a massive building program in Rome, filling the city with grand buildings and statues. His aim was to make the city look like the capital of a great empire. He commissioned new basilicas (meeting halls), temples, triumphal arches and a new Senate House, as well as repairing old buildings. In one year alone, 82 of the city's temples were faced with gleaming new white marble. Augustus decided that the Forum, Rome's center of law, government and business, was too small and overcrowded for the growing population. A new Forum was built and named "Forum Augustum" after the emperor. This impressive building program was designed to win support from the Roman people.

TRIUMPHAL ARCH

Augustus erected triumphal arches to celebrate military victories and other achievements. He built this one in 19 BC to mark a diplomatic treaty made with Rome's eastern enemies, the Parthians.

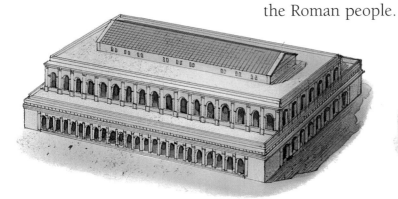

BASILICAS

A basilica was used for public gatherings and legal cases, and by bankers and businessmen. When Caesar's basilica burned down, Augustus rebuilt it on a grander scale.

CIRCUS MAXIMUS

The Circus Maximus was a huge racetrack, used for chariot racing. Augustus decorated its central spine with monuments, including an Egyptian obelisk (a four-sided stone pillar), a reminder that Augustus had added Egypt to the Roman Empire.

AQUEDUCTS

The city's water supply was carried in five huge aqueducts (water conveyors) from the River Anio and springs in the Anio valley. It flowed into holding tanks and then through pipes to bath-houses, public restrooms and drinking fountains. It also powered the city's flour mills. Augustus repaired all the old aqueducts and built a new one.

SLUMS

Although Augustus improved Rome's public buildings, most poor Romans continued to live in tall, overcrowded blocks of flats. These were often badly built. Packed close together in narrow streets, these timber-framed buildings were a constant fire hazard.

I found Rome a city of bricks, and I leave her clothed in marble.
AUGUSTUS

THE TEMPLE OF MARS THE AVENGER

The centerpiece of Augustus' new Forum was a temple dedicated to the god, "Mars Ultor," Mars the Avenger. Augustus had this built to celebrate his victory over the killers of Julius Caesar. He believed that the god Mars had helped him to avenge himself on his enemies. At the sides of the temple were statues of Rome's legendary founders, Aeneas and Romulus.

Augustus wanted to identify himself with these founders, claiming that, like them, he was beginning a new era for Rome. The north side of the Forum was lined with statues of Augustus' ancestors. He traced his family all the way back to Aeneas. On the south side, there were statues of other great Romans of the past.

PEOPLES OF THE EMPIRE

Within the Roman Empire there were three main groups of people – Roman citizens, *peregrini* (foreigners) and slaves. Peregrini had fewer rights than citizens. Slaves had no rights at all; they were property, like farm animals, and were even described as "living tools." The citizens were divided into different orders, or ranks. The senatorial order of aristocratic families was at the top. They provided Rome's senators, generals and provincial governors. The senators were millionaires, whose wealth came from vast farming estates. Below them was the less wealthy equestrian order, Rome's business class. At the bottom was the mass of ordinary citizens. Women had few political rights – they could not vote, speak in public meetings or hold office. Despite this, wealthy and aristocratic women could become very influential.

TOGAS

Only citizens were allowed to wear the long woolen toga. Equestrians wore a toga over a tunic with a narrow purple stripe, while senators had a tunic with a broad purple stripe. Magistrates and priests wore a toga edged with purple.

PEREGRINI

The peregrini were free non-citizens, who formed most of the population in the early empire. They paid higher taxes than citizens and were not allowed to vote. They could not serve as magistrates on their local councils and had fewer legal rights than citizens.

BECOMING A CITIZEN

Peregrini could serve in the Roman Army as auxiliary troops (see page 25). They were paid less than the citizen soldiers, the legionaries. But when they retired after 25 years' service, they became Roman citizens, a status they then passed on to their children.

AWARDS OF CITIZENSHIP

When the Romans conquered a new territory, such as Gaul, they gave citizenship to the local rulers to help win them over. The chieftains of Gaul became Romans, adopting Roman dress, learning Latin, and even taking a new Roman name.

THE SLAVE MARKET

Like almost all ancient societies, the Romans took slavery for granted. Slaves might be captured in war, bought from foreign peoples, or bred from slave parents.

THE CHAIN GANG

Conditions for slaves varied widely. Slaves who worked on the great farming estates had the hardest lives. They were often chained to stop them running away.

HOUSEHOLD SLAVES

Life was more comfortable for these slaves, often born in a Roman household. They grew up with their owners' children and were seen as part of the family.

FREED SLAVES

Long, loyal service was rewarded with freedom, and freed slaves were often set up in business by their former owners. Slaves could also earn money and save up to buy their freedom. They could then even become slave-owners themselves.

SLAVE WORK

Wealthy Romans relied on their slaves to do almost everything for them, from dressing them to carrying them through the streets on a litter. A litter was a form of transport where a person sat on a couch-like seat and was carried by slaves.

ATTITUDES TO ROMAN RULE

The Greeks had much in common with the Romans, worshipping the same gods, under different names. Many Greeks welcomed the peace and security of Roman rule.

A Greek

A Jew

The Jews were like a separate nation within the Roman Empire. They worshiped only one god, banned the use of religious images such as statues, and had strict rules about which foods they ate. The Romans could not understand why the Jews were so different, and many Jews hated the Romans. There were several uprisings against Roman rule, all brutally crushed.

TRADE

CARGO SHIP
This is a carving of a big-bellied Roman cargo ship. From March to November, these slow but sturdy wooden ships sailed on regular routes all around the Mediterranean, carrying large loads. Augustus cleared the seas of pirates, making it easier for ships to sail in safety.

After years of war, Augustus' rule brought peace to the lands around the Mediterranean Sea. This "Pax Augusta" (Peace of Augustus) was a great boost to trade. It became easier for traders to travel around the Roman Empire, carrying goods from one place to another. The Empire was also a rich market for luxury goods from distant lands, such as spices from India and silk from China. Another aid to trade was Augustus' coinage. During the civil wars, the rival generals had all issued their own coins, made of various metals. Augustus gave Rome a single currency, with standard values. People all over the Empire used the same copper, bronze, silver and gold coins. Augustus realized he could use his coins to announce his achievements and spread information.

ROMAN TRADE GOODS
This map shows some of the goods traded in the Roman Empire in the late first century AD. Goods traveled from many lands to Rome, and also from place to place within and beyond the Empire. To take just one example, Roman pottery, mass-produced in Italy, has been found in lands as far apart as Britain and India.

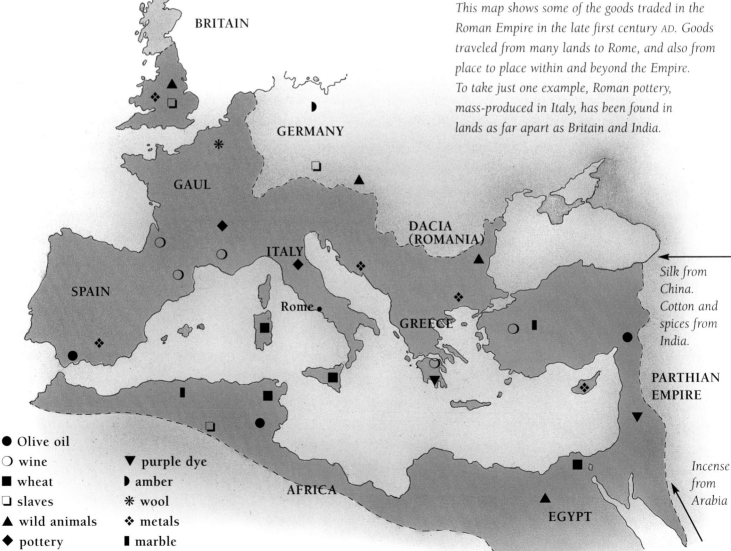

BRITAIN

GERMANY

GAUL

DACIA
(ROMANIA)

ITALY

SPAIN

Rome

GREECE

Silk from China. Cotton and spices from India.

PARTHIAN EMPIRE

AFRICA

EGYPT

Incense from Arabia

- ● Olive oil
- ○ wine
- ■ wheat
- ❏ slaves
- ▲ wild animals
- ◆ pottery
- ▼ purple dye
- ▶ amber
- ✳ wool
- ❖ metals
- ▮ marble

WEIGHING GRAIN

Every month, Augustus gave a free grain ration to every citizen in Rome. This mosaic from Rome's port, Ostia, depicts the grain being weighed. Giving the Roman people food was one way that Augustus kept them content with his rule.

THE EMPEROR'S COINS

Without newspapers, television or radio, coins were a good way to spread information to a large number of people quickly.

FATHER OF HIS COUNTRY

Every coin had a portrait of the emperor, showing people what their ruler looked like. This coin declared that Augustus was Pater Patriae (father of the country), a title given to him in 2 BC.

EGYPT CAPTURED

The crocodile, a famous Egyptian animal, stood for Egypt. The slogan underneath, which means "Egypt captured," announced Augustus' takeover of the country, following the suicide of Antony in 30 BC.

FOOD FOR EVERYONE

The ears of wheat on this coin from 27 BC were a symbol of plenty. They reminded people that Augustus was supplying them with cheap wheat from Egypt, which was governed by the emperor's representative.

RECOVERY OF THE STANDARDS

On this coin from 20 BC, the god Mars the Avenger holds Roman army standards (symbols). These had been captured years before by the Parthians. After Augustus made a treaty with Parthia, the standards were returned.

HIGH PRIEST

The Romans believed that every aspect of life was controlled by gods, ranging from small household gods, who watched over store cupboards and doorways, to Jupiter, "Best and Greatest," who protected the whole Roman Empire. Augustus was the "Pontifex Maximus," the chief priest of the Roman religion. It was his responsibility to offer sacrifices and prayers to the gods, to ensure their continued goodwill. Throughout the year, there was a series of festivals, each with its own set ceremonies. Each ritual had to be performed in a specific way to please the gods. For example, white cows were sacrificed to Juno, goddess of mothers, while Jupiter would "accept" only white bulls.

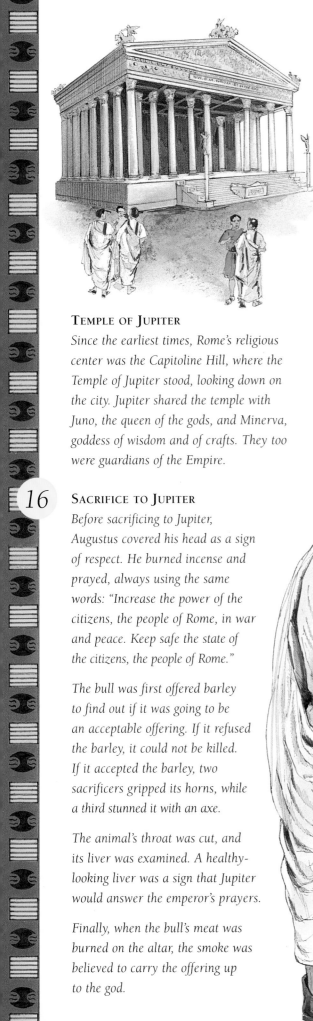

TEMPLE OF JUPITER

Since the earliest times, Rome's religious center was the Capitoline Hill, where the Temple of Jupiter stood, looking down on the city. Jupiter shared the temple with Juno, the queen of the gods, and Minerva, goddess of wisdom and of crafts. They too were guardians of the Empire.

16

SACRIFICE TO JUPITER

Before sacrificing to Jupiter, Augustus covered his head as a sign of respect. He burned incense and prayed, always using the same words: "Increase the power of the citizens, the people of Rome, in war and peace. Keep safe the state of the citizens, the people of Rome."

The bull was first offered barley to find out if it was going to be an acceptable offering. If it refused the barley, it could not be killed. If it accepted the barley, two sacrificers gripped its horns, while a third stunned it with an axe.

The animal's throat was cut, and its liver was examined. A healthy-looking liver was a sign that Jupiter would answer the emperor's prayers.

Finally, when the bull's meat was burned on the altar, the smoke was believed to carry the offering up to the god.

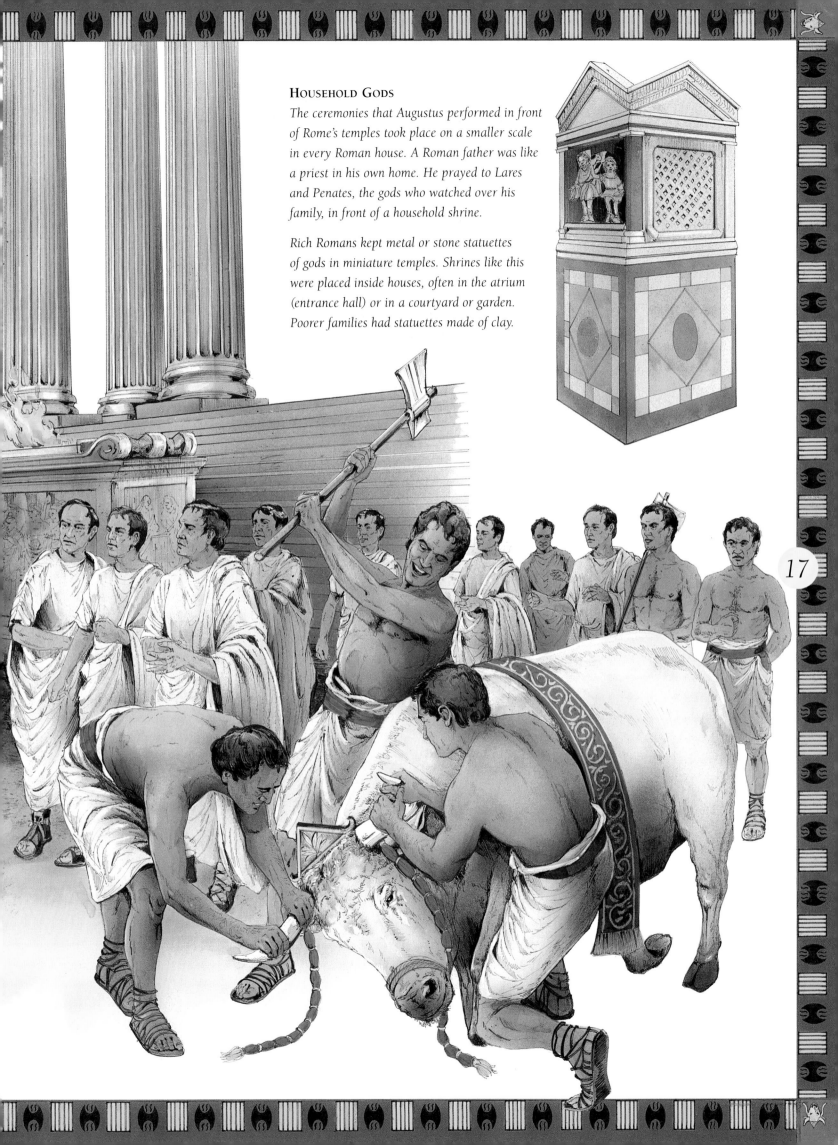

HOUSEHOLD GODS

The ceremonies that Augustus performed in front of Rome's temples took place on a smaller scale in every Roman house. A Roman father was like a priest in his own home. He prayed to Lares and Penates, the gods who watched over his family, in front of a household shrine.

Rich Romans kept metal or stone statuettes of gods in miniature temples. Shrines like this were placed inside houses, often in the atrium (entrance hall) or in a courtyard or garden. Poorer families had statuettes made of clay.

17

EMPEROR WORSHIP

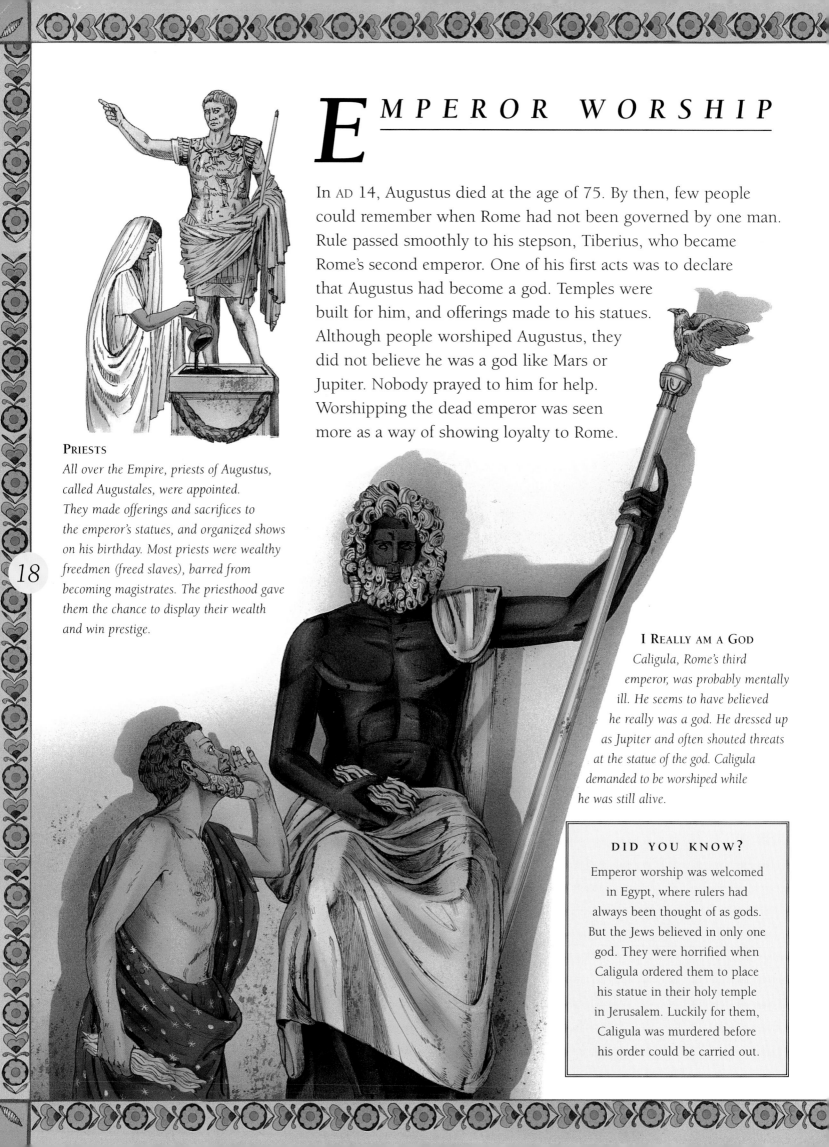

In AD 14, Augustus died at the age of 75. By then, few people could remember when Rome had not been governed by one man. Rule passed smoothly to his stepson, Tiberius, who became Rome's second emperor. One of his first acts was to declare that Augustus had become a god. Temples were built for him, and offerings made to his statues. Although people worshiped Augustus, they did not believe he was a god like Mars or Jupiter. Nobody prayed to him for help. Worshipping the dead emperor was seen more as a way of showing loyalty to Rome.

PRIESTS

All over the Empire, priests of Augustus, called Augustales, were appointed. They made offerings and sacrifices to the emperor's statues, and organized shows on his birthday. Most priests were wealthy freedmen (freed slaves), barred from becoming magistrates. The priesthood gave them the chance to display their wealth and win prestige.

18

I REALLY AM A GOD

Caligula, Rome's third emperor, was probably mentally ill. He seems to have believed he really was a god. He dressed up as Jupiter and often shouted threats at the statue of the god. Caligula demanded to be worshiped while he was still alive.

DID YOU KNOW?

Emperor worship was welcomed in Egypt, where rulers had always been thought of as gods. But the Jews believed in only one god. They were horrified when Caligula ordered them to place his statue in their holy temple in Jerusalem. Luckily for them, Caligula was murdered before his order could be carried out.

BECOMING A GOD

The Romans invented a spectacular ceremony for turning their dead emperors into gods. It was called a "consecratio," which means transferring something from our world to the world of the gods. This ivory plaque shows a consecration ceremony.

Read the captions from the **bottom upwards** to follow the proper sequence of events.

WELCOME TO HEAVEN

Gods, and other dead emperors who have become gods, welcome the new arrival to Heaven. The figure on the right with the shining halo is Helios, the sun god.

JOURNEY TO HEAVEN

The emperor is carried upwards by two wind gods. The sky is shown by the signs of the zodiac on the right.

THE RELEASE OF THE EAGLES

The new emperor has set fire to the pyre. As the flames rise, eagles are released, to symbolize the dead emperor's soul soaring up to heaven.

THE FUNERAL PYRE

This funeral pyre is a wooden structure draped with cloth and decorated with a statue. Augustus' body was placed inside his pyre and burned. Later emperors were buried, and wax effigies of them were burned in the pyre.

THE EMPEROR BECOMES A GOD

A big statue of the emperor sits in the miniature temple. This shows the people that he is now to be worshiped as a god.

THE FUNERAL PROCESSION

A great procession marches around the dead emperor's funeral pyre. It includes a carriage, like a carnival float, pulled by a team of elephants. A miniature temple sits on top of the carriage. Officials, riding in chariots, wearing masks of dead emperors, also take part (these are not shown in this picture).

FUNERAL COINS

People who did not attend the ceremony could learn about it from coins. This coin gives a clear view of the emperor's pyre, draped with cloth and covered with statues.

20

NERO'S MOTHER, AGRIPPINA

Powerful and ambitious, Agrippina hoped to rule the Empire through her son. She was so important at the start of Nero's reign that she even appeared alongside him on Roman coins.

THE SINGING EMPEROR

Nero believed that he was a magnificent poet, musician and singer. He went to Greece, saying, "The Greeks alone are worthy of my genius. They really listen to music!"

His Greek audiences loved their singing emperor, but Rome's upper classes were shocked by his behavior.

N ERO

The last ruler from the family of Augustus was Nero, who became emperor in AD 54. He owed his position to his mother, Agrippina, who was Augustus' great granddaughter. She had married the previous ruler, her own uncle Claudius, and persuaded him to adopt Nero, her son by a previous marriage. She then poisoned her husband, and Nero became emperor, aged just 16. At first, he was guided by his mother. But as he grew older, Nero wanted to break free of her influence. In AD 59, he had his mother stabbed to death. With Agrippina out of the way, Nero felt free to indulge his real interests – music and chariot racing. He set off on a musical tour of Greece, where he sang in competitions, always winning first prize. He even won the chariot race at the Olympic Games, although he fell out of his chariot before the end of the race.

THE GOLDEN HOUSE

In AD 64, a terrible fire destroyed the center of Rome. Nero seized the opportunity to build himself a vast palace, the "Domus Aurea" (Golden House). Towering over the entrance was a 40 yard-high bronze statue of the emperor, his head crowned with rays, like a sun god. The Romans resented Nero's palace and suspected him of starting the fire himself.

A SHOWER OF PETALS

When Nero first saw his new home, he said, "At last I can begin to live like a human being." The dining room ceiling had panels that slid back, to allow rose petals or perfume to be sprinkled on his guests below.

NERO'S DOWNFALL

In AD 65, Nero learned of a plot to overthrow him. Suspecting everyone, he had dozens of leading Romans arrested and executed. This led to a widespread rebellion in AD 68, when senators and military commanders rose against him. Abandoned by everyone, Nero killed himself, saying, "What an artist the world is losing!"

GREAT SHOWS

Nero's suicide was followed by civil war, with four Roman emperors ruling in quick succession. The final victor was Vespasian, an old general, who founded a new dynasty, the Flavians. He tore down Nero's hated Golden House and began building a vast amphitheater on the site. It was opened in AD 80 by his son, the emperor Titus, who organized a free spectacular and bloodthirsty show for 50,000 people. First, they saw thousands of wild animals being driven into the arena and killed. Then they watched fights between gladiators – slaves trained to fight to the death.

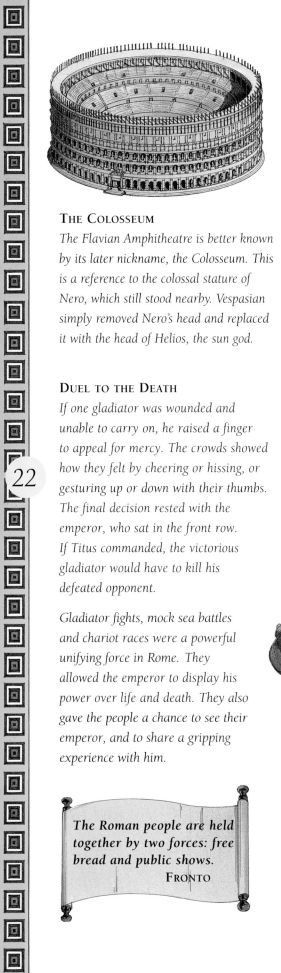

THE COLOSSEUM

The Flavian Amphitheatre is better known by its later nickname, the Colosseum. This is a reference to the colossal stature of Nero, which still stood nearby. Vespasian simply removed Nero's head and replaced it with the head of Helios, the sun god.

DUEL TO THE DEATH

If one gladiator was wounded and unable to carry on, he raised a finger to appeal for mercy. The crowds showed how they felt by cheering or hissing, or gesturing up or down with their thumbs. The final decision rested with the emperor, who sat in the front row. If Titus commanded, the victorious gladiator would have to kill his defeated opponent.

Gladiator fights, mock sea battles and chariot races were a powerful unifying force in Rome. They allowed the emperor to display his power over life and death. They also gave the people a chance to see their emperor, and to share a gripping experience with him.

The Roman people are held together by two forces: free bread and public shows.
FRONTO

22

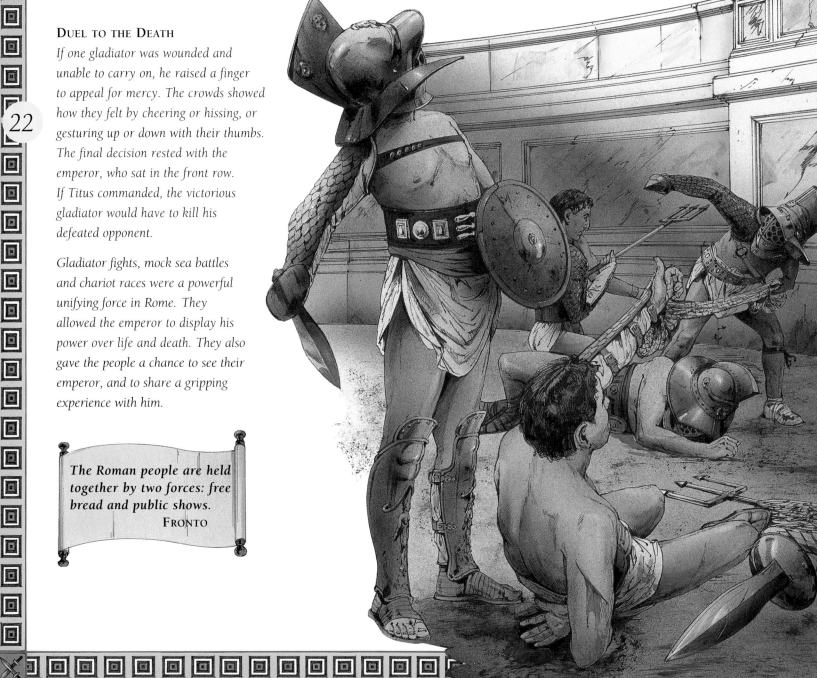

CHARIOT RACES

Rome's largest chariot racetrack, the Circus Maximus (see page 10), could hold around 255,000 spectators. The charioteers belonged to four teams, named after different colors, each with its own fanatical supporters. Fights often broke out between rival groups of fans.

COMMODUS

A later emperor, Commodus, was so obsessed with gladiators that he became one himself, even moving into the gladiators' barracks. He appeared in the Colosseum, dressed as the hero Hercules, and chased and killed ostriches.

DID YOU KNOW?

Wild animal shows demonstrated the emperor's ability to collect exotic animals from all over the known world and bring them to Rome. Killing them displayed the emperor's power over nature itself. This had a devastating effect on wildlife around the Empire. Lions were wiped out in Mesopotamia (Iraq) and the North African elephant became extinct.

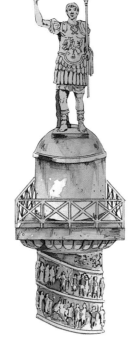

TRAJAN'S COLUMN

Trajan's column is decorated with a 225 yard-long spiral frieze, showing 2,500 figures in amazing detail. The emperor's statue stood on top. When he died, his ashes were placed in a tomb at the base of the column.

O N   C A M P A I G N

The word *emperor* comes from *imperator,* a Roman title for a military commander. The emperor was commander-in-chief of Rome's armies. It was his responsibility to protect the Empire and, if possible, to add new conquests. Of all the emperors, the greatest military general was Trajan, who ruled from AD 98–117. Trajan spent much of his reign at war, conquering Dacia (Romania) and part of the Parthian Empire. With these conquests, the Roman Empire reached its greatest size. After his death, Trajan's eastern conquests were abandoned by the next emperor, Hadrian. Trajan commemorated his victories on a 40 yard-high marble column in Rome. The carvings of scenes from his Dacian wars are a wonderful visual record of Roman army tactics and equipment. They show soldiers on the march, crossing rivers, building camps, tending the wounded and going into battle. The emperor appears in many scenes, addressing his troops and sacrificing to the gods.

TRAJAN'S TRIUMPH

After his conquest of Dacia, Trajan held a victory parade, called a triumph, through Rome. The streets were packed with cheering crowds. Everyone in Rome wanted to see the emperor and his victorious soldiers march past.

> **The Roman people owe the conquest of the world to no other cause than military training, discipline in their camps and practice in warfare.**
> VEGETIUS, *Military Science*

Marching near the emperor's chariot were attendants called lictors. They always accompanied the emperor when he appeared in public. Each lictor carried a bundle of rods and an axe. Originally, lictors were the attendants of magistrates, such as consuls. The rods and axe symbolized the magistrate's power to have people beaten or killed.

Dressed in a purple and gold toga, the emperor rode in a golden chariot. A slave held a laurel wreath over his head and repeated the words, "Remember, you are just a man". This was to avoid angering Jupiter, who was believed to punish the overly proud.

THE ROMAN ARMY

The most important soldiers of the Roman Army were the legionaries – Roman citizens who wore heavy armor and fought on foot. Fighting alongside them were non-citizen specialist fighters, known as auxiliaries.

ON THE MARCH

Each legionary marched long distances, carrying 40 pounds of equipment.

A slinger

An archer

AUXILIARIES

The auxiliaries included Syrian archers and slingers from islands off Spain. They were usually sent into battle first, raining missiles on the enemy. Then the legionaries moved in to fight at close quarters.

THE TORTOISE

At a trumpet signal, the highly trained legionaries could link their shields above their heads to form a "testudo" (tortoise). This protected them when attacking a fortification or when fighting uphill.

25

Soldiers carried important Dacian prisoners on a wooden platform. Above the prisoners was a display of their weapons hanging from a pole. At the end of the triumph, the prisoners were usually executed and the weapons placed in the Temple of Mars the Avenger.

The triumph included white oxen, draped with embroidered cloth strips, led by sacrificers carrying axes. The procession made its way up the Capitoline Hill to the Temple of Jupiter. Here the oxen were sacrificed to thank Jupiter for giving the Romans victory.

MILESTONES

Milestones like this have been found all over the Roman Empire. Each stone was inscribed with the name of the emperor who built or repaired the stretch of road and the distance to Rome or the nearest big city.

The Emperor Caesar Nerva Trajan Augustus Germanicus... father of his country, consul three times, built this road by cutting through mountains and getting rid of the curves.
Written on one of emperor Trajan's milestones, AD *100*

R OADS

There were few permanent roads before the Romans conquered their Empire. Mostly, there were trackways, which turned to mud in wet weather, or when troops with horses and carts marched along them. To help the army move quickly from place to place, the Romans built a network of firm roads, which could be used in all types of weather. Speed of movement was crucial, so a straight route was usually chosen, even if this meant tunneling through a hillside, or spanning a valley with a long bridge called a viaduct. The road network helped to keep the peace. Official mounted messengers could quickly carry news of rebellions or invasions to the emperor and the Army could reach any trouble spot within a couple of days. Thus, Roman roads both deterred peoples of the Empire from rebelling against Roman rule, and foreign enemies from invading.

SURVEYING THE ROUTE

Military surveyors plotted the routes of roads, using a tool called a groma. This was a wooden pole topped with a cross, with plumb lines hanging from the arms.

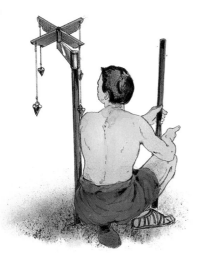

Using a groma

Carrying a kerb stone

Stamping down sand

Spreading sand

SOLDIERS AT WORK

*Roads were built by Roman soldiers and, in peacetime,
roadbuilding was seen as a useful way of keeping them fit
and busy. Historians know that the soldiers themselves
hated this work, because they complained
about it in their letters.*

Carrying gravel

**Spreading
gravel**

**Laying
a paving
stone**

**Setting
a kerb stone**

Viaduct

FIRM FOUNDATIONS

*Roman roads were built to last, with deep, firm foundations. The soldiers dug a
trench and then packed it with layers of sand, gravel and different-sized stones set
in cement. The surface was either paved with hard stone, or covered with gravel,
depending upon what was locally available. A sloping surface helped drain
rain water into side ditches.*

OFFICIAL MESSENGERS

*Official messengers galloped along the roads, carrying
news and the emperor's orders. Every 10 miles or so
there was a post house, where a messenger could
exchamge his tired horse for a fresh one. In an
emergency, it was possible for news to travel 150
miles in one day.*

IMPERIAL JOURNEYS

Although Rome was the capital of the Empire, the emperor did not need to spend all his time there. Many emperors went on long journeys, visiting the different provinces. The greatest traveler of all was Hadrian, who spent more than 12 years away from Rome, on journeys that took him to every part of his empire. Hadrian believed that the Empire had grown too big, and decided that there should be no more wars of conquest. With this policy, he risked losing the support of the soldiers, who relied on wars for wealth and glory. One reason Hadrian traveled so much was to visit the frontier armies, to ensure they remained loyal to him.

HADRIAN'S WALL

Hadrian kept his soldiers busy building frontier defenses. When he visited Britain, he made the army build a 67-mile wall across the country, from coast to coast.

THE EMPEROR IS HERE!

Excited crowds gathered to cheer Hadrian as he rode through the streets of their city. The people might have spent months preparing for the visit, organizing food supplies and entertainment, and writing speeches of welcome. They would talk about the visit for years afterwards.

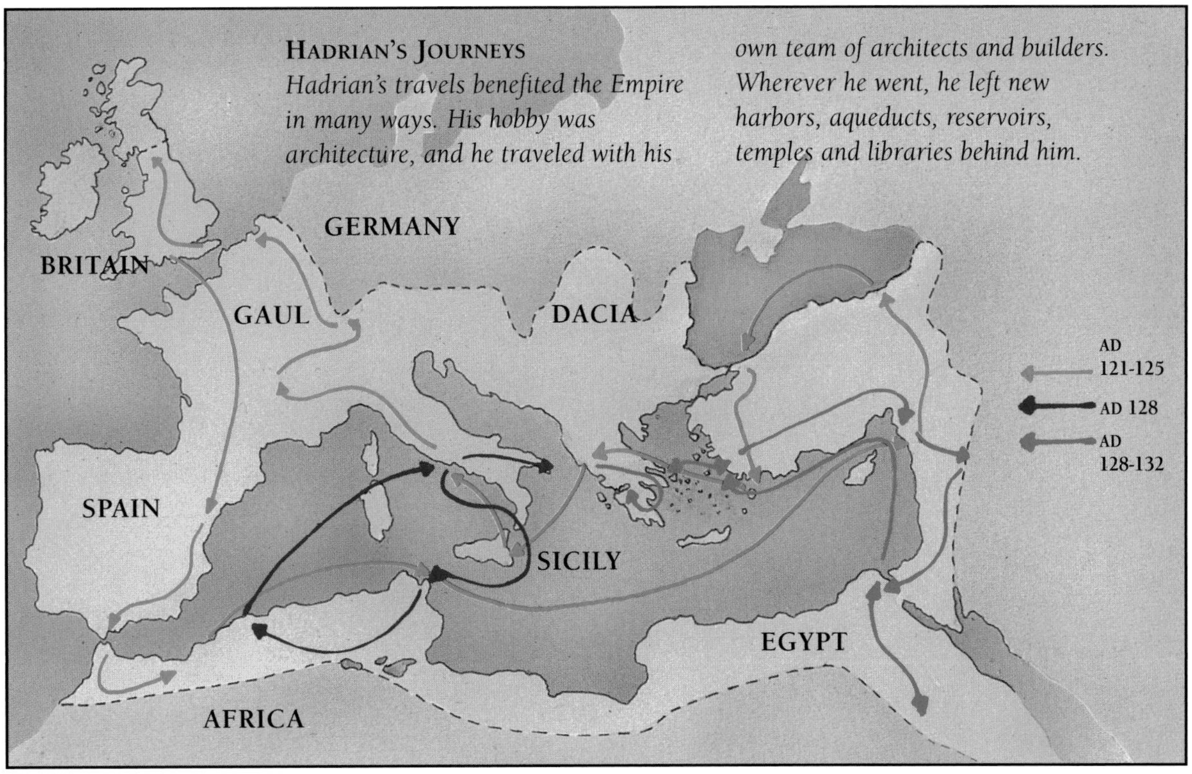
BRITAIN
GERMANY
GAUL
DACIA
SPAIN
SICILY
EGYPT
AFRICA
AD 121-125
AD 128
AD 128-132

Hadrian's Journeys
Hadrian's travels benefited the Empire in many ways. His hobby was architecture, and he traveled with his own team of architects and builders. Wherever he went, he left new harbors, aqueducts, reservoirs, temples and libraries behind him.

Distributing Money
On arrival at a city, the emperor distributed money to the local people, who pressed forward to see the most powerful man in the world. It was also a chance for them to hand him petitions asking for favors, such as the right to be Roman citizens.

DID YOU KNOW?

According to a Greek historian, a woman once stopped Hadrian and asked to speak to him. He replied that he had no time. The woman retorted, "Then don't be emperor!" Shaken by her words, he listened to her request. This story was also told of Greek kings, but it shows what people expected of their rulers.

BATHS OF CARACALLA

CARACALLA

Caracalla was a ruthless man who murdered his younger brother and co-emperor, Geta, along with thousands of his followers. Building a bathhouse was an attempt to make himself popular. He, in turn, was assassinated by one of his own soldiers.

One way in which emperors tried to win the love of their people was by building bathhouses. Far more than merely a place to wash, a bathhouse was a social center, where people spent their afternoons relaxing and socializing with friends. Romans could not imagine life without bathhouses and every town in the Empire had at least one for the local people. Five emperors built vast bathhouses in Rome, each outdoing the earlier builders both in scale and expense. One of the largest was built by Caracalla, who ruled the Empire from AD 211–217. It could hold more than 1,500 people at once.

CARACALLA'S BATHS

Caracalla's impressive bathhouse sprawled over 11 hectares on the outskirts of Rome. Surrounding the cold, warm and hot baths were libraries, gardens, restaurants, shops and a running track. The interiors were richly decorated with mosaics and marble.

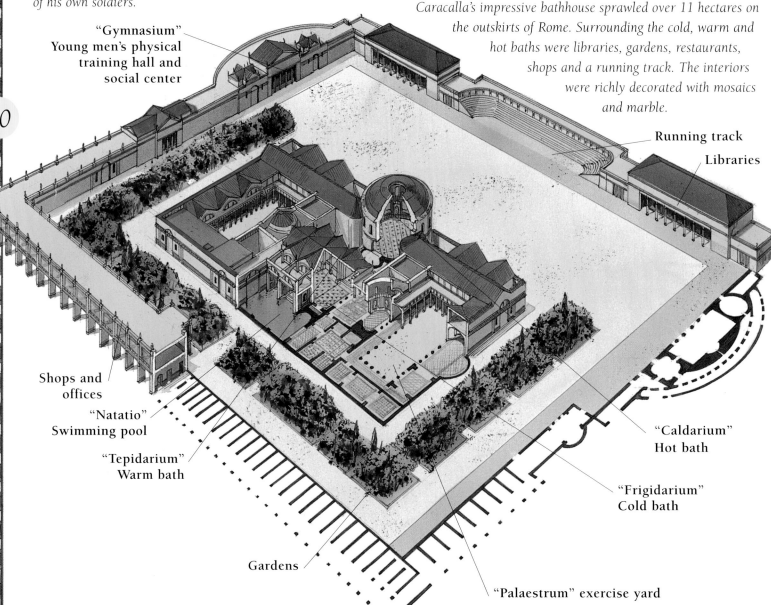

"Gymnasium"
Young men's physical training hall and social center

Running track

Libraries

Shops and offices

"Natatio"
Swimming pool

"Tepidarium"
Warm bath

"Caldarium"
Hot bath

"Frigidarium"
Cold bath

Gardens

"Palaestrum" exercise yard

EXERCISING

People often began a visit to the baths with exercise in the two palaestra (exercise yards). Men wrestled, lifted lead weights and played ball games. Women played a ball game with a hooked stick, like hockey, and some also wrestled.

LIBRARY

Less energetic visitors could read books or scrolls in the bath's libraries. Texts were written by hand on long rolls made from papyrus leaves or fine animal skins. Books with separate pages, a Roman invention, were beginning to be used in Caracalla's time.

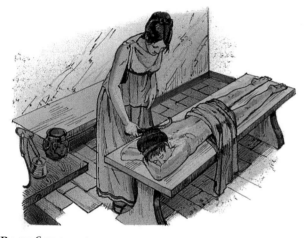

BACK SCRAPING

The baths were staffed by slaves, who stoked the furnaces with wood, carried towels and gave massages to the bathers. This slave has rubbed perfumed olive oil on a woman's back. She scrapes it off with a curved metal scraper, called a strigil.

SWEATING

The hot bath included sudatoria, or sweating rooms. Some were steam baths. Others used dry heat, with hot air passing through spaces under the floor and behind the walls. The bathers wore wooden shoes to protect their feet from the heated floors.

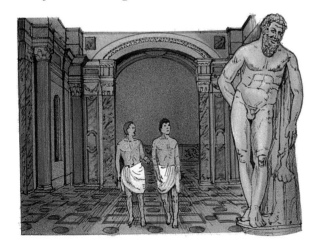

ADMIRING THE ART

The halls of the baths were lined with marble statues of gods, heroes and emperors, for people to admire as they strolled and chatted. Statues from Caracalla's baths can still be seen in Naples museum.

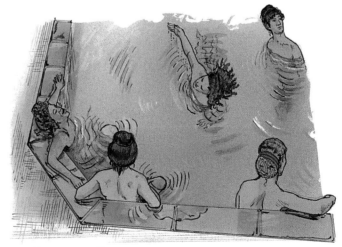

SWIMMING POOL

Caracalla's baths had a huge open-air swimming pool, where bathers could finish off their visit with a refreshing dip. The pool was emptied several times a day and refilled with clean water from a reservoir.

31

EMPIRE IN TROUBLE

In the middle of the third century AD, the Roman Empire was under attack from several sides. Germanic peoples – Goths, Vandals and Franks – broke through the frontiers in the north. From the East came the threat of a new, aggressive Persian Empire. A succession of Roman emperors failed to provide effective leadership. Between AD 235–284, there were 21 official rulers and many more pretenders. Almost all of these emperors died violently after short reigns, most of them murdered by their own troops. The worst humiliation of all took place in AD 260, when a Roman emperor was captured in battle by the Persians. He was never seen again. The same year, the western provinces broke away to form a separate empire.

THE AURELIAN WALL

Faced with invasions, many Roman cities built defensive walls. Even Rome was given a wall, by the emperor Aurelian, in AD 271. Aurelian was an effective leader, but his wall was a sign of the Empire's weakness.

32

THE GOTHS

The Goths invaded from the north, overrunning Dacia, which was lost to the Empire. In AD 251, they defeated and killed the emperor Decius in battle. Seventeen years later, they invaded Greece and destroyed Athens.

THE PERSIANS

Rome's old eastern enemies, the Parthians, had been overthrown by the Persians in the AD 220s. The new Persian Empire became Rome's most dangerous enemy. Led by King Shapur I, the Persian Army sacked the cities of the East, such as Antioch. Shapur boasted, "We ravaged and conquered them, taking their people captive."

THE EMPEROR WHO WAS STUFFED
In AD 260, the emperor Valerian was captured in battle by the Persians. It was said that King Shapur used Valerian as his mounting block. When the emperor died, still in captivity, his body was stuffed with straw and displayed in a Persian temple.

THE WEST BREAKS AWAY
By AD 260, the Westerners had lost patience with their emperor's failure to defend them. Following the capture of Valerian, Postumus, governor of Lower Germany, seized power in the west. He created a miniature Roman Empire, complete with a Senate and capital city, Trier. For eight years, Postumus defended his empire against both the Germanic invaders and the official emperor, Gallienus. He was eventually killed by his own troops.

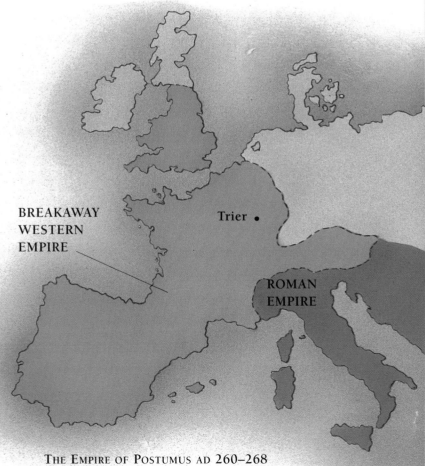

BREAKAWAY
WESTERN
EMPIRE

Trier •

ROMAN
EMPIRE

THE EMPIRE OF POSTUMUS AD 260–268

Postumus

DIOCLETIAN

From the AD 270s, the Roman Empire made a slow recovery. A series of soldier emperors beat off Rome's enemies and stabilized the frontiers. They were men of humble birth, who had risen through the ranks of the army. The greatest was Diocletian, proclaimed emperor by his troops in AD 284. Realizing that the Empire was too big to be ruled by one man, Diocletian appointed a partner, Maximian, to govern the west. Each of these two "Augusti" had a junior emperor, called a "Caesar." Diocletian restructured the Empire, doubling the number of provinces from 50 to 100. The governors of these new, smaller provinces did not have the military resources to start rebellions. This system lasted for 21 years. In AD 305, Diocletian retired, the only Roman emperor ever to give up power voluntarily.

THE TETRARCHS

Diocletian and his partners were known as the tetrarchs (four rulers). This statue shows the tetrarchs gripping their eagle-hilted swords and clasping each other tightly – a powerful image of strength and unity.

34

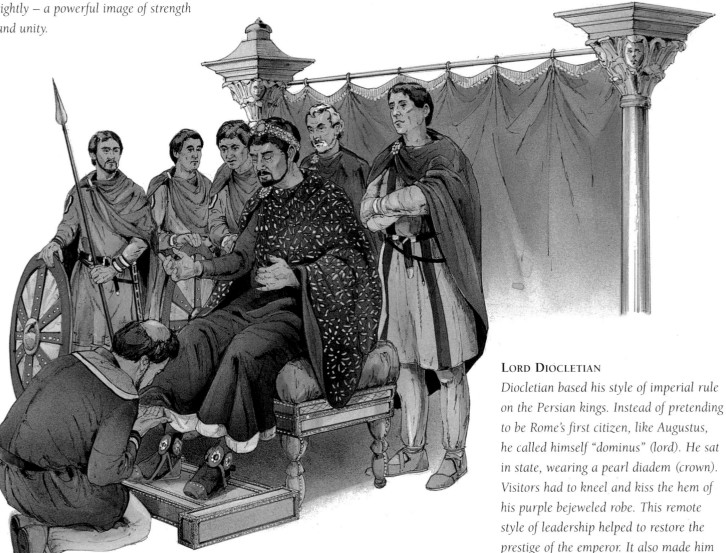

LORD DIOCLETIAN

Diocletian based his style of imperial rule on the Persian kings. Instead of pretending to be Rome's first citizen, like Augustus, he called himself "dominus" (lord). He sat in state, wearing a pearl diadem (crown). Visitors had to kneel and kiss the hem of his purple bejeweled robe. This remote style of leadership helped to restore the prestige of the emperor. It also made him harder to assassinate.

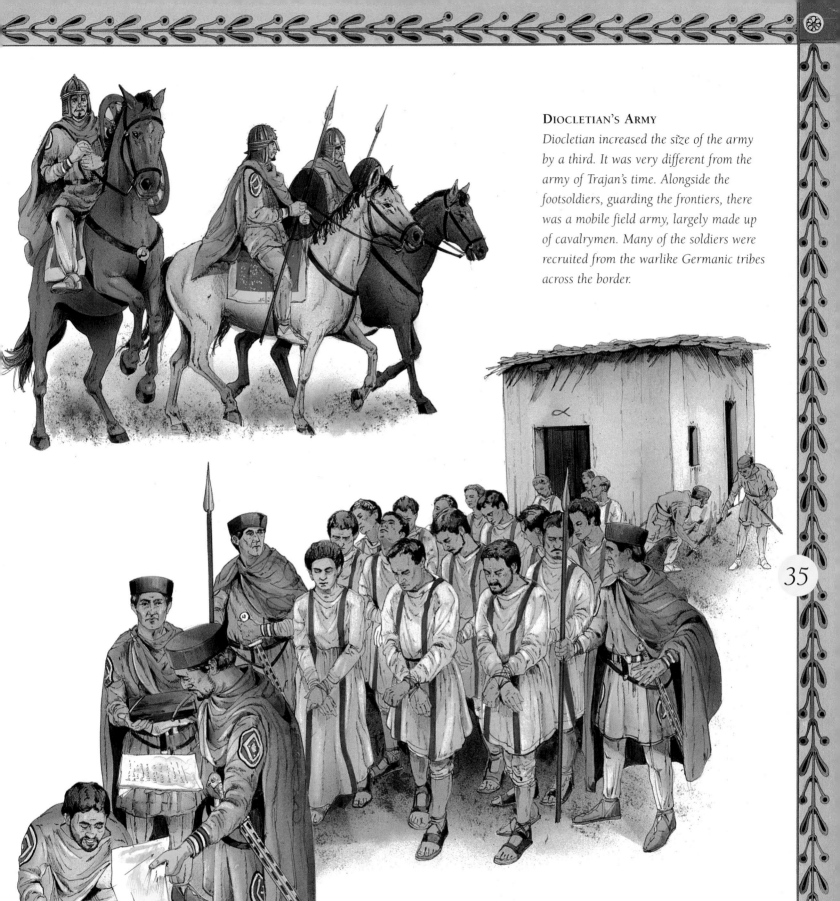

DIOCLETIAN'S ARMY

Diocletian increased the size of the army by a third. It was very different from the army of Trajan's time. Alongside the footsoldiers, guarding the frontiers, there was a mobile field army, largely made up of cavalrymen. Many of the soldiers were recruited from the warlike Germanic tribes across the border.

PERSECUTING THE CHRISTIANS

Jesus Christ was a Jewish preacher, executed by the Romans sometime around AD 30. Christ's followers claimed that he had risen from the dead, and they began to preach a new religion, Christianity. By Diocletian's time, Christians were a minority living all over the Empire. The emperor saw the religion as a threat. Christians refused to worship Rome's gods, claiming that they were demons. Such behavior could only bring the anger of the gods down on the whole Empire. In AD 303, Diocletian began a massive persecution of Christians. Their books and meeting places were burned. Thousands were tortured and killed, preferring to die rather than sacrifice to the Roman gods.

CONSTANTINE

After Diocletian retired in AD 305, his system of government broke down, and the tetrarchs went to war with each other. The final victor was Constantine, who had become a Christian. When he marched on Rome to fight his rival, Maxentius, he claimed to have seen a vision of a Christian cross in the sky. He believed that his victory in the battle that followed was due to the help of Jesus Christ. Constantine did everything he could to spread his new religion. He turned the ancient city of Byzantium, in Greece, into a new Christian capital city, Constantinople. He built grand churches, and he appointed Christians to powerful positions at his court. For the Christians, who had been persecuted for years, this was an almost unbelievable turn of events.

CHRISTIAN SOLDIERS
Before his victory at the Battle of the Milvian Bridge, just north of Rome, in AD 312, Constantine made his soldiers paint the first two letters of 'Christ' in Greek – x (chi) and p (ro) – on their shields. This was a well-known Christian symbol.

THE CHURCH MEETS AT NICAEA
Christianity was very different from the old Roman religion. Worshipers of Jupiter and Mars rarely worried about what they believed. Their religion was simple: you offered sacrifices to the gods in return for their help.

Christians, on the other hand, had fierce arguments over their basic beliefs. For example, Jesus was thought to be both a man and God. What did this mean? Had he been God for all time or was he created by God at a moment in history? There were bitter arguments over these questions, with rival Christian groups calling each other maniacs, eels, cuttlefish and wolves.

In AD 325, Constantine brought 220 church leaders together at his palace in Nicaea. He forced them to agree on a common set of beliefs, called the "Nicene Creed". Intimidated by the emperor, only two refused to sign the document accepting the creed. The Nicene Creed did not end the arguments between Christian groups, but it laid down a set of beliefs still used today.

36

A ROMAN CHRIST

Constantine's idea of Jesus Christ was far removed from the original Jewish teacher. In this mosaic from Ravenna, Jesus is shown as a clean-shaven, Roman soldier, wearing the halo of the sun god. He is trampling on a lion and a serpent, which represent the forces of evil. Instead of a shield and spear, Jesus is armed with a cross and a book, bearing Christ's words in Latin, "I am the way, the truth and the life."

DID YOU KNOW?

Before becoming a Christian, Constantine worshiped the sun god Helios. He brought several features of sun worship into Christianity. Although nobody knew when Christ was born, Constantine decided to celebrate his birth in December, already celebrated as the birthday of the sun. He also declared that Sunday (the day of the sun) should be a day of rest.

NEW BUILDINGS FOR CHRISTIAN WORSHIP

Instead of worshiping in the open air, outside temples, as the Romans did, Christian worship took place indoors. The worshipers prayed, listened to readings from Christian books and shared a sacred meal of bread and wine – which stood for the body and blood of Christ.

This new way of worshiping called for a new kind of religious building. Constantine's churches were like temples turned inside out. The decoration and columns were on the inside, while the exteriors were plain.

Julian

Valentinian

Smashing the Gods

Most of the emperors who ruled after Constantine were also Christians, and they carried on his work of encouraging people to convert to their faith. The exception was Constantine's nephew, Julian. Although brought up a Christian, he secretly preferred the old Roman gods. When he became emperor in AD 361, he tried hard to revive the old Roman religion. He restored temples, appointed priests, and sacrificed thousands of animals to the gods. A talented writer, Julian wrote several works attacking Christianity, as well as a hymn to the sun god. However, before he could achieve anything lasting, Julian was killed in battle, fighting the Persians. After Julian, Christianity continued to spread. Valentinian I was a Christian, but he allowed people to follow any religion they chose. His son-in-law, Theodosius, banned all forms of pagan worship. All over the Empire, fanatical Christians destroyed temples and smashed statues of the gods.

JULIAN AND VALENTINIAN
"The gods command me to restore their worship," wrote the emperor Julian. But it was too late to stop Christianity. After Julian, Christian emperors, such as Valentinian, ruled. This bronze statue depicts him holding a cross, showing his Christian faith, and a globe, reflecting his image as world ruler.

38

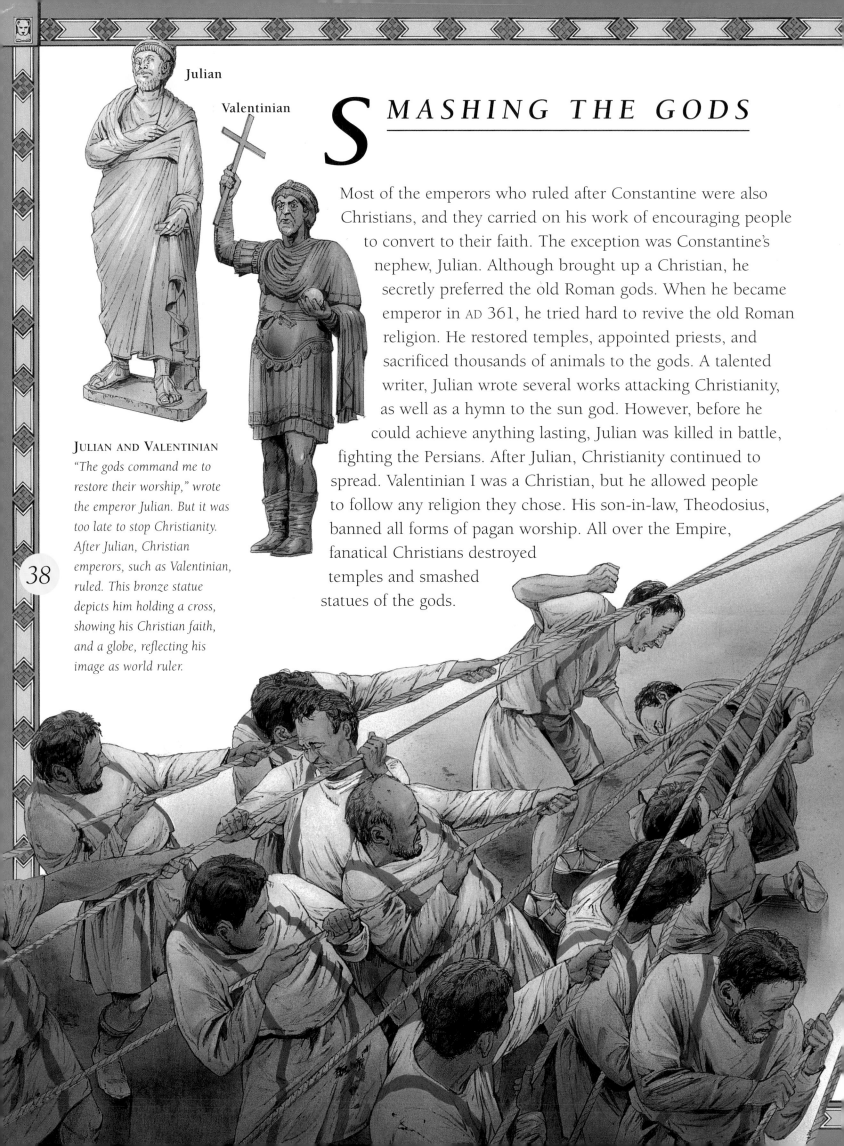

Mars

Saint Michael

The role of Mars, god of war, was taken
by Saint Michael, the warrior archangel.

GODS TO SAINTS

The Church used the cult of saints to win the
hearts of ordinary people. Roman gods were
replaced by Christian saints, who filled
similar roles, such as healing the sick.

DID YOU KNOW?

Not all the temples were destroyed.
Many of those still standing have
survived because they were
converted into churches. The best-
preserved Roman building
anywhere is the Pantheon in Rome.
This was a temple to all the gods,
built by the emperor Hadrian.
In AD 609, it was converted into
a church dedicated to Mary.
It is still a church today.

DESTROYING THE GODDESS ARTEMIS

*One of the most famous temples in the
Roman Empire was that of Artemis, at
Ephesus (now in Turkey). She was a Greek
nature goddess, known to the Romans as
Diana. Artemis had been worshipped at
Ephesus for over 1,000 years. Her temple
was one of the Seven Wonders of the
World. To the Christians, however,*
*she was a demon. In AD 401, a Christian
preacher, called John Chrysostom (golden-
mouthed), led an attack on the temple. The
priests watched in horror as the Christians
brought the statue of their goddess
crashing to the ground. Yet the Christians
were still nervous of her power. For
protection, they carved crosses all over
the walls of Ephesus.*

FALL OF THE WEST

After the AD 390s, the western half of the Empire began to fall apart. The northern frontiers collapsed and Germanic armies swarmed across Europe. Alaric, war chief of the Visigoths, led his army into Italy, sacking Rome in AD 410. After ravaging Italy, the Visigoths moved into southern Gaul. Meanwhile, the Vandals swept through Spain and into North Africa. Roman emperors made treaties with these invaders, allowing them to settle as "federates" – subjects, in theory, of the Empire. But they had their own kings, who blackmailed the emperors into giving them larger grants of land for their people. The western emperors ruled over shrinking territories, increasingly relying on Germanic soldiers to fight for them. In AD 476, Odoacer, a German officer, deposed the last emperor, Romulus Augustulus ("Little Augustus"). Odoacer declared himself King of Italy. Instead of a western Empire, there was now a patchwork of Germanic kingdoms.

A VANDAL LORD

We remember the Vandals in the word "vandalism," meaning mindless destruction. Yet the Germanic invaders did not intend to destroy the Roman way of life, only to share its wealth. The Vandal lord depicted in this mosaic looks like any rich Roman.

THE DESTRUCTION OF ROME

In AD 410, Alaric and his Visigoths spent three days attacking Rome, looting palaces, melting down golden statues and leading the people away as slaves. Rome was, by then, no longer the western capital. The imperial court had moved to the safety of Ravenna, which was protected by marshes. Nonetheless, the news of the destruction horrified people all over the Empire.

THE GERMANIC INVASIONS

In the AD 370s, the Huns, fierce horsemen from central Asia, attacked the eastern Germanic people, the Visigoths, who moved into the Roman Empire for refuge. They were followed by other Germanic tribes looking for land. Angles and Saxons crossed the sea to Britain and Ostrogoths conquered Italy. Franks and Burgundians invaded Gaul, driving the Visigoths into Spain.

Terrifying news has come to us from the West. Rome has been taken by assault. Sobs disturb my every word. The city has been conquered which had once ruled the whole world.

JEROME, *a monk in Palestine*

DID YOU KNOW?

The Germanic conquerors of the western Empire have left their names on our maps. The Angles gave their name to England, while France is named after the Franks. Lombardy, in northern Italy, takes its name from the Lombards. Burgundy, in France, is named after the Burgundians. The Vandals gave their name to Andalucia, in Spain. Gotland, in Sweden, was a home-land of the Goths. The Saxons are remembered in Saxony, in Germany.

BYZANTINE EMPIRE

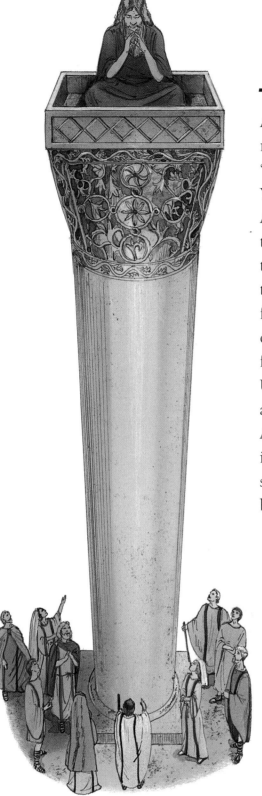

Although the west fell, the eastern half of the Empire survived for more than a thousand years. The eastern Empire was called "Byzantine," after Byzantium, the original name for Constantinople. Yet the Byzantines still thought of themselves as Romans, heirs to Augustus. Much about their lives would have seemed strange to that emperor. The Byzantines were devout Christians, who went to great lengths to be closer to God. Thousands withdrew from the world to live in monasteries. Some went further, living in caves, or even on the top of tall pillars. Byzantine emperors never forgot about the lost western territories. Under Justinian the Great, Byzantine armies even reconquered Italy, North Africa and part of Spain. After his death in AD 565, Justinian's conquests were soon lost. More lasting were the buildings he left in Constantinople.

RELIGIOUS PROCESSIONS
Much of the emperor's time was spent in elaborate religious ceremonies. Justinian and his wife, Theodora, led bishops and other churchmen on processions through the Church of the Holy Wisdom in Constantinople. They carried icons (images of Christ and the saints painted on wood) and holy relics, including a piece of the cross on which Christ had died.

LIVING ON A PILLAR
Simeon Stylites (AD 387–459) was a Syrian holy man, who spent 36 years living on top of a tall pillar. Simeon hoped to escape from the world's distractions, and commune with God. However, his pillar was constantly surrounded by sightseers and pilgrims, including emperors, who came asking for his advice.

The church has become a sight of marvelous beauty, overwhelming those who see it.
PROCOPIUS

THE LARGEST CHURCH IN THE WORLD

When it was built in AD 532–537, Justinian's Church of Hagia Sophia (Holy Wisdom) was the largest church in the world, with the widest and highest dome ever constructed. Its interior was covered with colored marble and mosaics, which glittered when the sun's rays streamed through the windows.

THE LEGACY OF ROME

We still live in the world created by the Roman emperors. We use the Roman alphabet and many Latin words. Our abbreviations, such as "e.g." and "etc," are of Latin phrases. We are surrounded by buildings inspired by Roman architecture. The Romans gave us many of our customs, including festivals, birthday parties and weddings. Roman brides dressed in white, carried flowers and wore a ring on the same finger people use today. The Roman legacy is so important in our lives that it is easy to take it for granted. Here are just a few of the ways in which we are still influenced by ancient Rome.

The Latin Language
The French, Spanish, Portuguese, Italian and Romanian languages all grew out of Latin and are called "Romance" languages. English is a Germanic language, but it has taken on thousands of Latin words over the years. Look again at the opening paragraph above. It contains 17 words derived from Latin, not counting "Roman" and "Latin". These are:

created	*creare*
emperors	*imperator*
use	*usus*
abbreviations	*abbreviare*
surrounded	*super* and *undare*
inspired	*inspirare*
architecture	*architectura*
including	*includere*
festivals	*festivalis*
parties	*partire*
carried	*carrus*
flowers	*floris*
same	*similis*
legacy	*legare*
important	*importare*
influenced	*influentia*
ancient	*antianus*

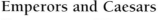

The Church
After the fall of the western Empire, the Christian Church kept alive many Roman traditions, including the Latin language and literature. Latin became an international language, used by scientists and scholars. Robes, still worn today by Catholic and Anglican bishops, are based on late Roman costume. The head of the Catholic Church, the Pope, is still called the "Pontifex Maximus", which means the chief priest.

Politics and Law
The Roman legacy includes the legal and political systems of many Western countries. Our legal systems were influenced by the Body of Civil Law drawn up by the emperor Justinian. The United States of America is one of several republics based on the Roman Republic. Americans have a Senate and use the Roman eagle as their emblem.

Emperors and Caesars
For centuries, Western rulers copied the style and titles of Roman emperors. The 19th-century French ruler, Napoleon, styled himself "consul" and then "l'impereur" – he was even crowned with a gold laurel wreath. Until the early 1900s, Germany and Austria were each ruled by "kaisers," and Russia by a "tsar." Both titles are versions of "caesar." The word "prince" comes from Augustus' title "princeps," while "palace" refers to Palatium, the hill in Rome where the early emperors lived. "Duke" comes from the late Roman military title "dux."

Architecture

Many public buildings, such as town halls, libraries and museums, are based on the style of Roman temples. In the 19th century, many countries imitated Roman imperial architecture, with triumphal arches and imposing statues of rulers and generals. Domestic architecture also owes a lot to the Romans, who were the first people to use bricks and tiles on a large scale. Yet another legacy is concrete, a Roman invention.

Roman Cities

All over Europe, people still live in cities founded by the Romans. Roman cities included London and York in England; Paris, Lyons, Toulouse and Arles in France; Cordoba, Toledo, Seville, Merida and Tarragona in Spain, and Cologne, Augsburg and Trier in Germany.

Roman Roads

Roman roads lasted without needing repair for hundreds of years after the Empire fell. In Europe, people still travel along the routes of many Roman roads.

Running Water

The Romans were experts in the control of water – building aqueducts, pipes, public toilets and sewers. The aqueduct at Segovia in Spain is still used today.

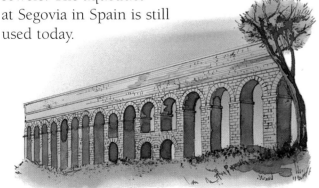

Swimming Pools

Next time you visit a swimming pool, think of its ancestor, the Roman bathhouse.

The Calendar

We still use the Roman calendar. Most months are named after gods, such as Mars (March) and Juno (June), but two take their names from Roman rulers. July is Julius Caesar's month and August is named after Augustus.

Mars

Julius Caesar

The Planets and the Week

The names of the Roman gods Jupiter, Venus, Mars, Mercury and Saturn were given to the planets. The Romans thought there were seven planets, including the Moon and Sun, and this is the origin of the seven-day week. Each day was thought to be influenced by a different planet.

Jupiter

Coins

All over the world, people use money based on Roman coins. In the United States, as in ancient Rome, coins depict admired leaders, as well as the Latin phrase "E pluribus Unum ("out of many, one").

Books

Even this book is a Roman invention. The Romans were the first people to use books with separate pages, rather than a long scroll.

WHO'S WHO

Pompey
(BORN 106 BC. DIED 48 BC)
Pompey was Rome's most successful general in the first century BC. He won a war against King Mithridates of Pontus and brought Syria into the Roman Empire. He was awarded the surname Magnus (the Great). However, his rivalry with Julius Caesar led to civil war.

Julius Caesar (BORN C.100 BC. DIED 44 BC)

An ambitious politician and general who conquered Gaul and then used his army to seize power in Rome. After making himself dictator for life, he was assassinated in the Senate. All Roman emperors adopted his surname, Caesar.

Mark Antony (BORN 82 BC. DIED 30 BC)
Julius Caesar's friend and lieutenant in his wars. Antony was the leading man in Rome following Caesar's death. His rivalry with Octavian led to another civil war, and his subsequent suicide in Egypt.

Augustus
(BORN 63 BC.
RULER 31 BC–AD 14)
Octavian, renamed Augustus, was Rome's first emperor. A far-sighted statesman, he invented a new system of government, the principate. He disguised his total power by pretending he had restored the Republic. Augustus' long reign got Romans used to the idea of being ruled by one man.

Tiberius (REIGNED AD 14–37)
Augustus' stepson, Tiberius, was Rome's second emperor. Moody and difficult, he found it hard to work with the senators. He hated their flattery and often remarked about them as he left the Senate, "Men fit to be slaves!" He spent the last years of his reign living in seclusion on the island of Capri.

Caligula (REIGNED AD 37–41)
Gaius, nicknamed Caligula ("little boots") was the greatgrandson of both Augustus and Mark Antony. At first he was popular, but he began to behave in an increasingly peculiar manner. Caligula believed he was a god, and threatened to make his favorite horse, Incitatus, a Roman consul. He was stabbed to death by members of the imperial guard.

Claudius (REIGNED AD 41–54)
Caligula's uncle, Claudius, was handicapped by bad health. He drooled, stammered and suffered from nervous tics. To improve his public image, Claudius organized the conquest of Britain in AD 43. He was also a prolific writer, who composed histories, a book on the Roman alphabet and an autobiography.

Nero
(REIGNED AD 54–68)
Nero was notorious for murdering his mother, stepbrother and two wives. Terrified of plots, Nero had many leading Romans executed. When he was finally overthrown, there was nobody left from Augustus' family left to succeed him.

Vespasian (REIGNED AD 69–79)
A successful general, Vespasian made himself emperor after winning a civil war against his rival, Vitellius. He established the Flavian dynasty, which ruled Rome for 27 years.

Titus (REIGNED AD 79–81)
Eldest son of Vespasian. His short reign saw a number of disasters, including a plague, a great fire in Rome, and the eruption of Mount Vesuvius, the volcano which buried the town of Pompeii. Titus completed and opened the Flavian Amphitheatre, which became nicknamed the Colosseum.

Domitian (REIGNED AD 81–96)
Vespasian's second son was another tyrant, like Nero. He fell out with Rome's ruling classes, and had many senators executed for plotting against him. It was said that he liked to spend hours alone in his room, catching flies and stabbing them with his pen. Eventually, a group of plotters, including his wife, was able to murder him.

Trajan (REIGNED AD 98–117)
Trajan was the first of the "adoptive" emperors, who ruled between AD 98 and 180. Each emperor adopted a leading Roman as his son, to succeed him. The first emperor from outside Italy, Trajan came from an Italian family who had settled in Spain. A great military leader, Trajan's conquests brought the Empire to its greatest size.

Hadrian (REIGNED AD 117–138)

Hadrian was the second Spanish emperor. He never felt at home in Rome and spent much of his reign traveling around the Empire. He gave up Trajan's eastern conquests and built frontier defenses, such as Hadrian's Wall across Britain.

Marcus Aurelius (REIGNED AD 161–180)

Marcus Aurelius was kept busy fighting defensive wars against the Germanic tribes. A philosopher as well as a general, he wrote *The Meditations*, one of the most famous books ever written by a monarch.

Commodus (REIGNED AD 180–192)

Marcus Aurelius was the first emperor since Vespasian with a son to succeed him. The reign of his son, Commodus, showed again the problem of hereditary succession. Commodus was a bloodthirsty man, who wanted to be a famous gladiator. He was eventually strangled by his wrestling trainer.

Septimius Severus (REIGNED AD 193–211)

Septimius Severus was a North African, who founded another dynasty of emperors, the Severans. A ruthless general, he won power following another civil war. On his deathbed he said to his two sons, "Keep on good terms with each other, be generous to the soldiers, and ignore everyone else."

Caracalla (REIGNED AD 211–217)

The elder son of Septimius Severus, who murdered his younger brother, Geta, making himself sole ruler. His most famous act was to make all free people in the Empire Roman citizens.

Valerian (REIGNED AD 253–260)

Valerian ruled at a disastrous time – when the Empire was under attack from Persians and Germanic tribes. Campaigning against the Persian king, he was tricked into attending a meeting, where he was captured. He died a prisoner of the Persians.

Postumus (REIGNED AD 260–80)

For eight years, Postumus was ruler of a breakaway western empire. He was killed by his own troops when he refused to allow them to destroy Mainz.

Aurelian (REIGNED AD 270–275)

Aurelian was one of the soldier emperors of the late third century. He came from a poor family, and rose through the ranks of the army. Aurelian was a good general, nicknamed "sword in hand." Like most of the emperors of the time, he was eventually killed by his soldiers.

Diocletian (REIGNED AD 284–305)

A brilliant statesman and tireless organizer, Diocletian changed the way the Empire was ruled, appointing three co-emperors to share the burden. He strengthened the army, and restructured the provinces. After 21 years, he retired voluntarily to a huge palace on the coast of Dalmatia (modern Croatia), where he devoted himself to growing cabbages.

Constantine the Great

(REIGNED AD 306–337)

The first Christian emperor, Constantine was convinced he had been chosen by God to spread his faith. He built a new Christian capital, Constantinople. A ruthless man, he executed his own wife and eldest son, believing they were plotting against him.

Julian (REIGNED AD 361–363)

Julian was nicknamed the "apostate," which means "renegade from his faith." He rejected Christianity and tried to restore the worship of the old Roman gods. Julian died fighting the Persians, although it was said that he had been stabbed by one of his own Christian soldiers.

Valentinian I (REIGNED AD 364–375)

Valentinian was a successful general who established a dynasty of emperors. His family ruled over Rome for 91 years. Multi-talented, Valentinian was also a skilled painter, sculptor and inventor.

Justinian (REIGNED AD 527–65)

Justinian was the Byzantine emperor who tried to restore the old Roman Empire. His armies recovered Africa from the Vandals and overthrew the Ostrogothic kingdom of Italy. He was also famous for his building projects and his system of Roman law.

INDEX